GLIMPSE OF A RAINBOW

Poems by A.J

Glimpse of a Rainbow

First published 2022
This second edition published 2023
Text copyright © A.J 2023
Internal illustrations by Victoria Rusyn

All rights reserved. Apart from any fair dealing for the purposes of private study, research, criticism or review, as permitted under the Copyright Act, no part of this publication may be reproduced by any process or by any means whatsoever without written permission of the Author

A.J

LOSS

A.J

Glimpse of a Rainbow

To think
we would've known everything
about each other
and then knew nothing
is the biggest heartache of all

A.J

The first positive pregnancy test
I said
we're going to be parents
I'll never say that again
when I see those two lines
Only until
our baby is crying in our arms
is when I'll believe it

Glimpse of a Rainbow

My heart was the first thing
to react to seeing the blood
I stood up
The only thing I felt
was the hammering of it
Like the wings of a bird
desperately
trying to escape its cage

A.J

When you left
You took a piece of me with you
I like to think you still have it
It's yours to keep
It's a gentle, warm part of me
I hope it feels like a plush comfort
A soft feather
A streak of light beam
A burning candle
Without it, I'm not myself
But I'd rather you have it

Mothers Day

I've had glimpses of motherhood love
I saw your heart flicker
I imagined what you'd look like
I held you in me
I loved you and thought of you every day
but Mothers Day is not my day
and it feels slightly cruel
to experience a mother's love
but have no recognition for it

A.J

Your baby book should've
been filled with
My round belly
Your hospital bracelet
Gummy smiles
and notes on first giggles
Instead
I tied the ribbon closed
when only two pages were filled out
and it broke me to write *goodbye*

Glimpse of a Rainbow

Something hardened
in me that day
and I've been trying
to soften ever since
but at least hard
means less chance
of being hurt

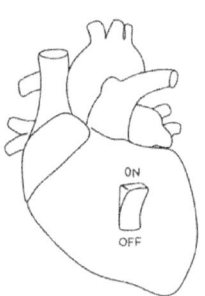

A.J

I can cope
with the ups and downs
of trying to become parents
The one thing I can't cope with
is the idea of never being a parent

Glimpse of a Rainbow

Your due date came and went
as normal as the first day of spring
I went to work
I watered your plant
No one called me
asking if there were any signs you were coming
I wasn't drinking raspberry leaf tea
or eating five dates a day
and you certainly weren't in my arms
I wasn't big and uncomfortable either
I was still small and empty

A.J

I wasn't a good person
the second time I miscarried
I was angry
Bitter
Like someone
wrapping their knuckles
gearing for a fight
Because I was
My fight to motherhood

Glimpse of a Rainbow

Drops of blood
on the toilet bowl
Like tears
from an injured eye

A.J

The flowers filled our home
I held them, instead of you

Glimpse of a Rainbow

The hardest thing to accept
Is there's no reason why you're not here
No reason to why my heart
will always yearn for you
and why I can't have you

A.J

Things change after a miscarriage
A sieve isn't just a kitchen utensil
A loose flowy dress isn't just for the beach
Pull-up pads aren't just for postpartum
It's not only your innocence
around pregnancy that's damaged
The everyday things are tainted, too

Glimpse of a Rainbow

I grieve you in the past we could've had
The present you're not here for
And for the future we will never share

A.J

The first ultrasound
You were attached to me
on the side of my womb
On the second ultrasound
you were floating in the middle
of a boundless sea
Not needing me

Glimpse of a Rainbow

To my friends

Even if you make a mistake
Are careless with your words
All I'm really thinking about
is how glad I am you don't understand
and how I hope you never do

A.J

My Before and After

It occurred on the plastic seats
in the outdoor dining area
BBQs on either side
Camping equipment laid out
I'd been somewhere like this before
Ready to be told what my day at school camp entailed
Kicking out my feet
Two ft shorter
My only problem being I was homesick
'I'm sorry, sweetheart, are you missing your family?'
Fifteen years later
My phone rang on the table
I gave one last look around
Knowing it may be the last time
that they were just camping facilities
and reminded me of nothing more
I hunched over
Two ft shorter again
as my doctor's soft voice filled the air around me
'I'm sorry, sweetheart, your pregnancy won't continue'

Waiting room

I'm sitting here
with the other mothers
I am less than
Without a bump
Without a heartbeat
Without contractions
Without any evidence I'm like them
It might be the loneliest feeling there is

A.J

Multiverse

In another space and time
I'm sitting with you
You're on my knee
here on this couch
In this universe
I'm here alone
In both, my eyes are spacey
Staring at the same spot on the carpet
In a multiverse, I'm tired from your tears
In this one, I'm tired from my tears
I'm not sure if it's just a thought
or if it's torture
to know there may be a version out there
where you're here with me

Glimpse of a Rainbow

Siblings

I wonder if your souls will
come back to me
In the meantime
I hope you're at least
somewhere together

A.J

If I could tell my babies one thing

You came here from love
and you left with the same
Not a moment we didn't love you
or you weren't protected
The world can be harsh
and it brings me some solace
you never knew pain

HEALING

A.J

Glimpse of a Rainbow

My first pregnancy

You put me on the path to motherhood
The first time we had a positive test
The first time we told people I'm pregnant
The first time I saw a heartbeat inside me
You'll never get to hear these stories
But your memories won't ever go to waste
I'll hold them near me till the day I die

A.J

My second pregnancy

I wish I could've celebrated your existence more
But I had to shield myself
from the heartbreak of another loss
I hope you know
I wanted you desperately
Even though I guessed you may leave

Glimpse of a Rainbow

I'm both scared of
not falling pregnant
and falling pregnant

A.J

My body

A home once so familiar
Every cushion worn and comfortable
Each wall known by fingertips
Then like waking up after an earthquake
Everything's misplaced and strewn around
and you can't see past the damage
It's how I saw my body
after the second time I miscarried

Invisible mother

Have you ever seen an invisible mother?
She still wants to be seen
And to be heard
But her pain is silent
And her child is not beside her
You know her from her glazed eyes
Not from sleeplessness of interrupted nights
But from chasing her dream
You know her by the way
She looks at a newborn
Desperate for what she almost had
You know her by her weary heart
That she still tries to present whole
Even when she's broken in half
An invisible mother
Is one without her child
Yet still a mother

A.J

You left my physical body
Yet you'll never leave my heart
And in that way
You will live on forever

Silver linings

It feels cruel to say there are positives to loss
I can't help but acknowledge
my deeper appreciation for
the ebbs and flows of life
The strengthened intertwine of our fingers
What I learnt about myself
and of strength
Trusting in the journey
A goal to work for
instead of it being handed to us
More excitement and joy
from family and friends
when the dream does come true
More appreciation of the miracle
that we fought a battle for

A.J

It was not my fault
your heart stopped beating
Yet
I can't help but be angry
my body didn't do the one thing
I wanted it to

Glimpse of a Rainbow

What I want other loss mamas to know

That it isn't your fault
You couldn't have prevented it
Your value isn't determined
by your ability to carry a baby
That you deserve grace
That you will be okay

A.J

Grieving
is like being cold
Arms seeking a jumper
and the sun comes out
Warmth spreads on your skin
The goosebumps disappear
Your skin smoothing
if only for a moment
And you know that
you won't be cold for long

Glimpse of a Rainbow

If it's a mother's responsibility
to preserve their child's memories
like keeping their
old toys and artwork
Then you'll forgive me for
talking about them
Reminiscing on the time
I was pregnant
It's the only memories of them
I'll ever have

A.J

Miscarriage and birth is
as close to nature
as women can get
We can't stop or prevent it
We have to watch it unfold
Like everything else in nature
Seemingly cruel sometimes
Natural, nonetheless

Glimpse of a Rainbow

If they weren't meant to be
we'd be happier without them
If they weren't meant to be
we wouldn't be in pain
Just because another baby
may come after them
doesn't mean
they weren't meant to be

A.J

Don't tell us 'at least'
Don't promise us it won't happen again
We don't need you to minimise our grief
We just need you to be there

Glimpse of a Rainbow

I feel ashamed
at how my stomach sinks
when there's an announcement
or when I see a scan picture
An empty feeling with the ghost of joy
It's not because I'm jealous
or just that I wish it was me
It's that in an alternate universe
it *is* me

A.J

Pregnancy loss
is the only way
to be a portal
between life and death

Glimpse of a Rainbow

What people don't understand
Is that my grief connects me to you
Grief is all I have left

A.J

'At least you can get pregnant'
Stings
Women do not get pregnant
for the sake of it
What's the use of pregnancy
without a baby in your arms

Glimpse of a Rainbow

When I'm asked if I have children
there's a second of pause
before the 'no'
Then my voice floats off
more answers on the tip of my tongue
an aftertaste of loss

A.J

I didn't get stretch marks
Yet my stomach still needed to heal
from the gaping hole
of the reality that
it no longer needed
to stretch to grow life

Glimpse of a Rainbow

Miscarriage is the exact moment
Your life will be split between
What is
And what could've been

A.J

After a large fire dissipates
The air turns yellow
and foggy
It's how I saw everything
after you left

HOPE

A.J

Glimpse of a Rainbow

It's a universal experience
Altered perspective
after a loss
It's as if the world is full of
Waddling women
Extended bellies
Pushing strollers
Swaddled babies
The way we see the world is not how it is
it's how *we* are
So notice other miracles too
The way waves crash differently
each time on the shore
The tender sound of a violin
playing your favourite song
How your soul lights up
when you watch the sunrise
Pregnancy may be a miracle
but there are miracles for us too

A.J

One day my pain will be physical
instead of emotional
I will swap an empty uterus
for an aching, healing one
I will swap quiet tears
for ones of overwhelm
I will swap a flat stomach
for one with evidence of life
One day
my heart will exist outside of my body
Still painful at times
But not like it is now

Glimpse of a Rainbow

The most confused I've been
on this journey
is when part of me was relieved
I wasn't pregnant
Pregnancy after loss is the
only thing where your
biggest dream comes true
yet it's the most terrifying
because at any second
without warning
it can be gone

A.J

I take note of the hard things
The things that mums talk about
I imagine them
as happy and innocent as fresh flowers
Piercing cries in my sleep
Stretched, sore skin
Bleeding nipples
Always being needed
Yawns as large as canyons
I collect them
like small pieces of paper
mums have thrown over their shoulder
I pin them to a board
whispering them like wishes
Imagining a time when all those hard things
will become mine, too
When I'm a mother

Glimpse of a Rainbow

Just relax

You tell me—
if you had the chance to have everything
you ever dreamt of
Would you relax
or would you be fighting for it

A.J

Hope
It's always there
Waiting for you to see
Ready to show you all that can be

Glimpse of a Rainbow

I relate to the way
a plant can push
through concrete
Defying physics
Finding a way
to reach its light

A.J

Birds still sing the same sweet song
The crackle of a fireplace still feels as warm
Dancing still frees my soul
In the waiting for you
life is still beautiful

Glimpse of a Rainbow

I'm not sure I believe
everything happens for a reason
I don't believe that
babies get robbed of a life
for a greater good
I believe that
humans are adept at finding
silver linings
and making the most
of bad situations
Isn't that far more beautiful
than things happening for a reason?

A.J

I will continue to fight
to fulfil my dream
I don't have another choice
I'm not going to live
in a world where I let
my dream loose
It's not as easy
as unfurling my fist
around the string
of a balloon
and letting it float away
It would mean the one life I have
would not be the one
I always envisioned

Glimpse of a Rainbow

My one wish
for the loss mamas
is to know softness
To not let it harden you
That whilst you seek
clarity or answers
you also seek light
Embrace the unknown
To know life
isn't meant to be easy
Even when it feels
like you're drowning
The tide will always bring you in

A.J

I think I'll only fully
breath again
once our baby
is in my arms
Until then
the air in my lungs
will be half still
and waiting

Glimpse of a Rainbow

As we pass gardens
we only see the flourishing flowers
We do not see the failed growth
of buds and small trees
The tears they cried
when their seeds didn't grow
Plenty of people suffer heartache
and struggle
We see only their blooming garden

A.J

Three or four kids would be the dream
we decided as teenagers
on a night laying in bed
As if it were so easy
Like planning to walk to the market
and pick out a perfect bunch of flowers

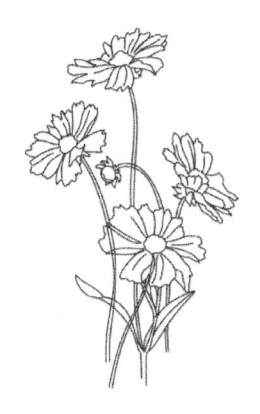

Glimpse of a Rainbow

Sometimes I feel a pang of guilt
that talking about miscarriage
may be shattering people's illusions
that pregnancy equals a baby
but
It's a thousand times better
to shatter an illusion
and be afraid of a possibility
than to never see it coming
and have it shatter you

A.J

I often think about
how I will look back on this time
Whether I talk about it much
Whether it becomes a defining period
I guess that all depends
on what happens next
It's hard to see how damaged
something will be
when you're still in the midst of the storm

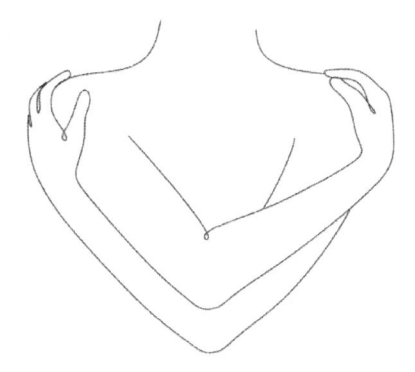

Glimpse of a Rainbow

I didn't think I'd feel happy
to see a positive test again
But the more time went on
the more hopeful I got
And the second time
we were very happy
I said that I will bring this baby home
That proves that things don't need
to be perfect the first time around
You can endure pain
and still have hope
It can still be beautiful
I know the third time I see a positive
will be beautiful too

A.J

The Two-Week-Wait
is another way of
life being measured in days

Glimpse of a Rainbow

My love for my angels did not encompass
physical or sentimental values
I had no clue
what colour eyes they'd have
or if their laugh was loud or meek
I couldn't know what
birthmark would be my favourite
one to kiss
I loved them for simply existing
The purest a love can get

A.J

Loss is the only thing I know
A positive test always fades
A scan always shows a weak heartbeat
or one that has stopped
So I hope my future child
can forgive me
for seeming blasé
during my pregnancy
That I wasn't as joyful to find out I was pregnant
That I didn't start a journal entry right away
That I didn't take early bump pictures
That I waited so long to buy you your first outfit
It's not that I wasn't excited
I was just terrified

Glimpse of a Rainbow

I miss her sometimes
Who I was before
The one who clicked her tongue in sympathy
when she heard of someone's miscarriage
but didn't think it would happen to her
The one whose heart was pure
Who thought she could plan her life
Who had control of her desires
Who didn't think anything could come
between her dreams

Perspective

They see a couple
Carefree, without restraint
frolicking, joking
weaving in and out of the waves
They reminisce
when they were that free
We see a couple
sitting on the sand
The baby is crying
Their faces are tense
but their hands are as full as their hearts

Glimpse of a Rainbow

There is a disconnect I feel
to people who haven't experienced my loss
How could they ever understand
the extreme pain
of losing something you never truly had?

A.J

To my husband

Maybe I got so lucky in love
I had to be unlucky in this
And if that's a trade off
That you cannot be too lucky
in the balance of life
it would be one I'd accept

Glimpse of a Rainbow

I know now
That I have to let go
I have to trust my journey
Whatever that looks like
To have complete faith
It's not easy
but I still believe

A.J

I store up kisses for you
Whenever you feel far
It helps process the pain
Knowing that one day
My future self will give you
all those extra kisses
and say they are from
the version of me
who so badly dreamt of you

Glimpse of a Rainbow

I can almost taste it
The life I'll have in ten years
I'll first mention this time
to my children
in a passing comment
on the way home from sport practice perhaps
or tucking them in bed one night
I'll tell them that they are miracles
Because the road was rocky
to bring them here
I'll look back on this time
of yearning and heartache
and feel sorrow for a past self
and only thankfulness for today

A.J

Glimpse of a Rainbow

I have constant glimpses of you
I see you in the light between trees
I hear you between the beats of soft music
I feel you around us when we talk about you
You're already in my heart
One day I'll look in your eyes
For now
I have glimpses everywhere
They are what I hang onto until you're here

Glimpse of a Rainbow

A.J

Someday, when life has unfolded and expanded in ways you couldn't have imagined, you will look back on this uncertain time. You will wish peace and understanding for your past self, in such a way that only the future version of yourself can deliver. Awash yourself in that patience and peace. Know your future self is looking back and whispering, 'everything is going to be alright.'

I hope you enjoyed reading Glimpse of a Rainbow. I aim to support and validate women who have experienced pregnancy loss through my writing.

To join the community or get in touch, follow us on Instagram or TikTok @glimpseofarainbow

A.J x

Printed in Great Britain
by Amazon